How To Teach

Breaststroke

Basic technique drills, step-by-step lesson plans and everything in-between

A swimming teacher's definitive guide to teaching breaststroke swimming stroke

Mark Young

A Catalogue record for this book is available from the British Library

ISBN 9780995484238

Published by: Educate & Learn Publishing, Hertfordshire, UK

Graphics by Mark Young, courtesy of Poser V6.0

Design and typeset by Mark Young

Published in association with www.swim-teach.com

Note: This book is intended for guidance and support only. The material contained here should accompany additional course material set on an official swimming teaching course by an official Swimming Association. Neither the author nor the publisher can accept responsibility for any injury or loss sustained as a result of the use of this material.

Teaching · Learning · Achieving · *Professional Swimming Help Online*

Mark Young is a well-established swimming instructor with decades of experience teaching thousands of adults and children to swim. He has taken nervous, frightened children and adults with a fear of water and made them happy and confident swimmers. He has also turned many of average ability into advanced swimmers. This book draws on his experiences and countless successes to put together this simplistic systematic approach to teaching swimming.

Also by Mark Young

Teaching Guides
How To Be A Swimming Teacher
101 Swimming Lesson Plans
How To Teach Front Crawl
How To Teach Backstroke
How To Teach Butterfly

Learn to Swim Guides
The Complete Beginners Guide to Swimming
How To Swim Front Crawl
How To Swim Breaststroke
How To Swim Backstroke
How To Swim Butterfly
The Swimming Strokes Book

Contents

Introduction

Breaststroke is one of the most popular swimming strokes swum by adults recreationally. Despite being a technically tricky stroke to swim correctly, it uses the least energy out of the four basic swimming strokes, even when it is poorly swum. For this reason, it is the ideal swimming stroke to teach adult beginners.

What Makes A Good Teacher?

'A teacher is one who makes himself progressively unnecessary.'
Thomas Carruthers

What makes a good teacher?

A teacher is looked up to by their pupils as a role model and a source of knowledge and guidance. A teacher possesses several key characteristics that make him or her individual and it is these personal characteristics that can determine a teacher's level of success.

A good swimming teacher requires a wide range of qualities. You will probably be stronger in some areas than others and as you gain experience you will build your competence in all areas.

Teaching Qualities

To be a good teacher and role model to your pupils, you need to possess some essential qualities. These are:

Knowledge

Having sound knowledge of your subject gains you respect, not only from your pupils but from parents and other swimming teachers. You will need to keep your knowledge up to date and always admit when you don't know the answer, but make it your business to find out.

Empathy

Teaching swimming requires empathy on all levels. For example, the child who is scared and has every reason to be, the adult who is equally scared or even embarrassed, the child who is over-excited at the prospect of going in the pool and the child who is trying hard but not keeping up with the rest.

Patience

All of the above examples that require empathy will also test your patience. As a teacher, you have to accept that not everybody learns at the same rate. Children's behaviour and attention spans will also try your patience at times. Whatever is thrown at you, you must show patience and control at all times.

Control and Management

It goes without saying that you must have control over your class, especially with children in a pool. In the classroom at school, children know what is expected of them but this is not always the case in the swimming pool. Children have to be controlled for safety purposes as well as learning purposes.

If pupils are being unruly throughout the lesson then not only is the lesson unsafe, but they are not learning anything. The golden rule is to set out your stall early on to show them who is boss. That is not to say that you have to 'rule with fear', otherwise pupils will not want to have swimming lessons with you, just let those that step out of line know they have done so and that it will not be tolerated.

Effective Communication

As a teacher, your job is to pass on information effectively and clearly, and your ability to do this will determine how quickly your pupils learn. Knowledge of your subject is also essential, but how you convey that knowledge is far more important. You could be a world expert on the human body and the scientific principles behind swimming but if you are not able to pass that expertise onto eager-to- learn pupils clearly and concisely, then you are not a good teacher!

Basic Principles of Effective Communication

Positioning

Where you position yourself on the poolside will determine how well your pupils can see and hear you. Study the pool diagrams in the planning and organisation section for best practice.

Clarity

Passing information on clearly will ensure your pupils do exactly what you want them to.

Conciseness

Keep your teaching concise to avoid your pupils becoming confused or taking in the wrong pieces of information.

Accuracy

Your teaching has to be accurate as you will be copied, mimicked and quoted especially by children. Inaccuracy will result in your pupils not learning and in you gaining a reputation as a poor teacher.

Enthusiasm

A sure way to motivate your class and get results is to have an enthusiastic approach. Enthusiasm is infectious and if you are full of it when you teach, your pupils will put every effort into what you ask them to do.

Interest

If the content of what you teach is not interesting then your pupils will not listen and become distracted. Enthusiasm and interesting content go hand in hand, as one breeds the other. The most uninteresting subject can be made interesting with an injection of enthusiasm.

Appropriateness

The teaching points and practices you use will determine the success and outcome of the lesson. If your methods are not appropriate, the pupils do not learn and the lesson becomes pointless.

Two-way

Communication works both ways. Ask your pupils questions and listen carefully to those who answer and how they answer. Encourage them to ask you questions at appropriate times.

Slow progress in adults learning to swim is completely normal and should not be looked upon negatively.

As a swimming teacher, you can do a few things to help.

- Be calm, relaxed and informal in your teaching style. This approach will help to relax your adult and keep them at ease.
- Adjust your expectations accordingly.
- Take their limitations into account when planning. Exercises and drills that suit one swimmer may not work for another.
- Be flexible in your approach. For example, fins or hand paddles (usually used in advanced drills) can often benefit adult beginners, as long as they do not become reliant on them.
- Be sensitive to their frustrations and always be supportive and empathetic in your response.
- Above all, use plenty of praise to stimulate and maintain motivation. At the end of each lesson, pick out the parts they showed progress in and highlight them as achievements of the session, however small they may be.

Equipment

Equipment

Floats and kickboards

When used correctly, floats can help develop specific parts of breaststroke technique. They are suitable for non-swimmers to advanced swimmers and can be used by both adults and children.

Swimming teachers use floats as part of lessons for many different exercises. Non-swimmers can use them to strengthen, and established swimmers can use them to isolate and perfect technique.

For example, the weak non-swimmer can use two floats, one placed under each arm, to help strengthen their breaststroke leg kick. The floats will provide stability and help boost confidence whilst encouraging a fast and furious leg kick.

Advantages:

- Very versatile and can help enhance a wide range of swimming exercises.
- It can be used in addition to other aids.
- It can be used in place of different types of swimming aid to encourage progression and enhance strength and stamina.
- When used individually, floats can help gain leg or arm strength.
- Fine-tune technique by encouraging a swimmer to focus on a specific area of their swimming stroke.
- Cheap to buy and easy to store. Also easy to use with large groups.

-

Disadvantages:
- Not suitable for very young children or babies learning to swim as they require a degree of strength to hold.
- Require close supervision

Common Mistakes to Watch Out For

It's difficult to misuse a float because they are such a simple piece of swimming equipment. However, there are a couple of points to watch out for when using floats to teach children.

Firstly, it is common for children to grip the float too tightly, especially if they are nervous beginners. They squeeze the float in their hand, resulting in a very tired hand grip. They then focus away from the part of their swimming they are supposed to be concentrating on.

Secondly, it is common for children to bear their weight onto the float, causing it to submerge. The nervous beginner does this without thinking, as they attempt to climb above the water surface instead of lying on the surface. Reassuring them and helping them relax by advising them to "let the float support you" will go some way to assisting the children in getting the most out of swimming floats.

These common problems can take time to fix as the swimmer begins to learn how to relax and become comfortable in the water. As long as the teacher is aware and the swimmer is made aware, they can progress gradually.

Woggle or Noodle

One of the most popular buoyancy aids, the swimming noodle, is a simple polythene foam cylinder. One of the most useful and versatile floats to use when teaching swimming.

Sometimes called a 'woggle', it is cheap to make, cheap to buy and easy to use in large group swimming lessons.

The main advantage is that it provides a high level of support whilst at the same time allowing the swimmer movement of their arms and legs. The swimmer can learn and experience propulsion through the water from both the arms and the legs.

The noodle is very versatile and as it is not a fixed aid, it can be used and removed with ease. It can also add a sense of fun to swimming as it can be tucked under the arms on the front and the back as well as placed between the legs and used as a 'horse'. The noodle is ideal for beginners learning breaststroke technique.

Advantages and Disadvantages of a Swimming Noodle

Advantages:

- Provides a high level of support for children of all sizes.
- Gives a sense of independence in the water with the minimum of support.
- Allows freedom of movement.
- Boosts confidence in the nervous beginner.
- Able to support adult beginners
- Easy to fit and remove, so ideal for use in group swimming lessons.
- Allows freedom of movement.

Disadvantages:

- Limited or no use for advanced swimmers.
- Nervous swimmers can 'clamp' it between their body and their arms, restricting their arm action.
- Can cause very buoyant swimmers to tip forwards.

Pull Buoy

A pull buoy is a figure-eight shaped piece of solid foam used mainly by established and advanced swimmers.

It is placed between the legs in the upper thigh area to support the body so the swimmer can swim without kicking the legs. The pull buoy allows them to focus on other parts of their swimming stroke, such as arm or breathing techniques.

This swimming aid is most useful when learning and practising front crawl and backstroke techniques. Swimming teachers should note that using a pull-buoy as a teaching aid for breaststroke can stress the lower back due to the upper body lift when breathing. Use an alternative teaching aide where possible.

Competitive swimmers often use pull buoys during their training sessions. They are designed to restrict the use of the swimmer's lower body, causing a greater intensity on the arms and upper body.

Holding it between the legs by squeezing the thighs together also helps keep the lower body in a streamlined and efficient shape during the swim. By isolating the upper body, the swimmer can focus entirely on their arm and hand technique or breathing technique, whilst the float assists to keep the lower body afloat.

They also help strengthen the upper body and arms by eliminating the kick propulsion while helping to keep the body position correct in the water.

This type of swimming aid is available in a smaller size for younger swimmers and full size for adults.

Pull Buoy Advantages and Disadvantages

Advantages:

- Provide good isolation of the upper body whilst keeping the lower body buoyant.
- Ideal for work-outs and training and therefore for established and advanced swimmers.
- Increased core strength.
- Available in adult and junior sizes.

Disadvantages:

- Not suitable for non-swimmers and beginners.
- Can place undue stress on the lower back when used for breaststroke.

Sinkers

Sinkers are objects such as sticks, hoops and toys that sink to the bottom of the pool. They are a great way to teach children breath control by encouraging them to submerge.

Sinkers can be used in both shallow and deep water and vary in design to cater for a range of ages. Although their uses rarely target a specific swimming stroke, they can open up a vast range of contrasting and complementary activities.

To children, sinkers are the equivalent of toys, so a swimming teacher with a creative imagination can use them to spark excitement and get some fantastic results.

Hand Paddles

Hand paddles are used to develop power in the arms, chest, shoulders and back muscles. They come in the form of large plastic paddles that strap to the palms of the hands and prevent the water from passing through the fingers.

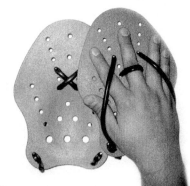

The swimmer can use hand paddles to enhance their feel for the water which will help to improve their breaststroke arm and hand technique.

Breaststroke Technique

Breaststroke

Breaststroke is the oldest and slowest of the four swimming strokes. It is also the most inefficient of all strokes, which is what makes it the slowest. Propulsion from the arms and legs is a consecutive action that takes place under the water. A significant frontal resistance area is created as the heels draw up towards the seat and the breathing technique inclines the body position, increasing resistance. These are the main reasons that make breaststroke inefficient and slow.

This stroke is usually one of the first strokes to be taught, especially to adults, as the head and face are clear of the water, giving the swimmer a greater perception of their whereabouts and buoyancy. There are variations in the overall technique, ranging from a slow recreational style to a more precise competitive style. Body position should be as flat and streamlined as possible with an inclination from the head to the feet so that the leg kick recovery takes place under the water.

The leg kick as a whole should be a simultaneous and flowing action, providing the majority of the propulsion.

The arm action should also be simultaneous and flowing. It provides the smallest propulsive phase of the four strokes.

The stroke action gives a natural body lift, which provides the ideal breathing point with each stroke. A streamlined body position during the timing sequence of the arm and leg action is essential to capitalise on the propulsive phases of the stroke.

Body Position

The body position should be inclined slightly downwards from the head to the feet.

The body should be as flat and streamlined as possible with an inclination from the head to the feet so that the leg kick recovery takes place under the water.
The swimmer's head movement should be minimal, and the shoulders should remain level throughout the stroke.

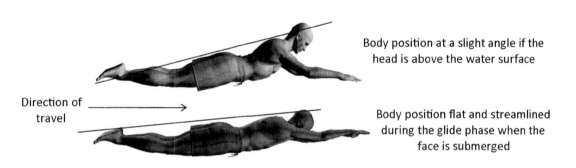

Body position at a slight angle if the head is above the water surface

Direction of travel

Body position flat and streamlined during the glide phase when the face is submerged

The main aim should be good streamlining, but the underwater recovery movements of the arms and legs and the lifting of the head to breathe compromise the overall body position. To reduce resistance created by these movements, as the propulsive phase of an arm pull or leg kick takes place, the opposite end of the body remains still and streamlined.

Common Body Position Mistakes

The most common mistake with the body position for breaststroke is being too flat in the water. In other words, the face is submerged too much, causing the hips, legs and feet to rise to the surface. This could then make lifting the face to the front to breathe more difficult. It could also lead to the feet breaking the water's surface as they kick and therefore losing power.

The angled body position can be perfected with a simple push and glide exercise. See the Breaststroke Exercises chapter for details on how to teach this.

Leg Kick

The essential teaching aspect of the legs is that the action is a series of movements that flow together to make one sweeping leg kicking action.

A swimmer or teacher needs to recognise the difference between the wedge kick and the whip kick in breaststroke. The leg action provides the most significant propulsion in the stroke, and swimmers will favour a wedge kick or a whip kick, depending on which comes most naturally. For a whip kick, the legs kick in a whip-like action with the knees remaining close together. For a wedge kick, the legs kick in a broader, more deliberate circular path.

  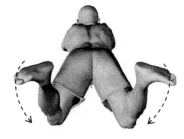

| Heels are drawn up towards the seat. Soles face upwards | Feet turn outwards to allow the heels and soles to aid propulsion | Heels push back and outwards in a whip-like action |

The leg kick as a whole should be a simultaneous and flowing action, providing the majority of the propulsion. Knees bend as the heels are drawn up towards the seat, and toes are turned out, ready for the heels and soles of the feet to drive the water backwards. The legs sweep outwards and slightly downwards in a flowing circular path, accelerating as they kick and return together and straight, resulting in a streamlined position.

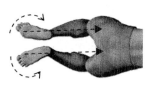

Heels drawn towards the seat and feet turn out

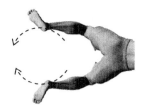

Heels drive back in a circular whip like action giving the kick power and motion

Kick finishes in a streamlined position with legs straight and toes pointed

Common Leg Kick Mistakes

The feet cause most of the problems when it comes to kicking. Failure to turn the feet out will result in a lack of power and a feeling of going nowhere. Inability to turn out both feet and only to turn out one foot will result in something known as a *screw kick*. This is where one leg kicks correctly and the other swings around, providing no propulsion at all.

The best exercise for correcting these common faults is to swim on your back (supine) with a woggle or noodle held under the arms for support. Kicking in slow motion at first, making a conscious effort to turn out both feet and ensure both legs and feet are symmetrical is best before attempting to add power. Then, the swimmer can sit up slightly and watch their leg kick as they perform it.

Arms

The amount of propulsion generated from the arm technique has developed over the years as the stroke has become more competitive. The overall arm action provides the smallest propulsive phase of the four competitive strokes.

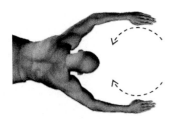

Arms and hands pull around and downwards

Elbows tuck in and arms and hands stretch forward into a glide

Catch

The arm action begins with the arms fully extended out in front, fingers and hands together. The hands pitch outwards and downwards to an angle of about 45 degrees at the start of the catch phase. The arms pull outwards and downwards until they are approximately shoulder-width apart. Elbows begin to bend, and shoulders roll inwards at the end of the catch phase.

Propulsive phase

The arms sweep downwards and inwards, and the hands pull to their deepest point. Elbows bend to 90 degrees and remain high. At the end of the down sweep, the hands sweep inwards and slightly upwards. Elbows tuck into the sides as the hands are pulled inwards towards the chest and the chin.

Recovery

The hands recover by stretching forwards in a streamlined position. Hands recover under, on or over the water surface, depending on the breaststroke style being taught.

The hand sweeps through the water downwards, inwards and then upwards. The elbow is high at the end of the down sweep and remains high throughout the in-sweep. The hand pulls through towards the thigh and upwards to the water surface.

Common Arm Technique Mistakes

The arm technique for this stroke usually becomes the dominant force when it should not. It is very common for swimmers to put more effort into pulling themselves through the water when the leg kick should provide the power and momentum.

In an attempt to haul them through the water, the arm pull is too big and wide. It is not uncommon to pull arms completely to the side, making for an inefficient recovery under the water surface, which will certainly result in the swimmer slowing down.

An easy exercise to practice to help perfect the arm pull technique is to walk slowly through water of about shoulder depth, ensuring the arms pull in small circles and the hands remain in front of the swimmer at all times. They should also extend forwards and remain there momentarily for the glide phase.

Breathing

Breaststroke has a natural body lift during the stroke, which gives the ideal breathing point during each stroke cycle.

Inhalation takes place at the end of the arm in-sweep as the body allows the head to lift clear of the water. The head should be lifted enough for the mouth to clear the surface and inhale, but not excessively to keep the frontal resistance created by this movement to a minimum.

The swimmer can utilise explosive or trickle breathing.
The head returns to the water to exhale as the arms stretch forward to begin their recovery phase.

Breathe IN

Breathing in occurs as the arms pull down and the head rises above the surface

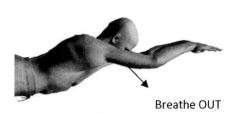

Breathe OUT

Breathing out occurs as the arms recover out in front

Some swimmers perform breaststroke with the head raised throughout to keep the mouth and nose clear of the water at all times. This simplifies the breathing but at the expense of more significant frontal resistance.

Common Breathing Mistakes

Some beginners experience difficulty breathing during breaststroke. The two main reasons are failing to lift the head enough to clear the water surface and breathe, and holding the breath and therefore failing to breathe out into the water.

Breaststroke needs a powerful leg kick, and it is this leg kick that gives a natural body lift. Together with the arm action, there should be enough lift to enable the mouth to clear the water surface for inhalation to take place.
The most common mistake made with breaststroke breathing is failing to exhale during the glide phase making it impossible to inhale again or forcing the swimmer to

use an explosive breathing technique.

Although explosive breathing is a valid breathing technique for this swimming stroke, it is usually only used competitively.

When swum recreationally, exhaling during the glide phase of the stroke is more efficient and uses less energy.

Using a woggle under the arms provides support and allows the swimmer to swim in slow motion while practising breathing. Extending the body into a long glide as exhalation takes place ensures the breathing takes place at the time that keeps the stroke at its most efficient.

Timing

The coordination of the propulsive phases should be a continuous alternating action, where one propulsive phase takes over as one ends. The stroke timing can be summed up with the following sequence: pull, breath, kick, glide.

A streamlined body position at the end of that sequence is essential to capitalise on the propulsive phases of the stroke. Breaststroke timing can be considered another way: when the arms are pulling in their propulsive phase, the legs are streamlined, and when the legs are kicking in propulsion, the arms are streamlined.

Full body extension is essential before the start of each stroke cycle.

Decreasing or even eliminating the glide and using the arm and leg actions in an almost continuous stroke to give more propulsion is a more competitive variation of stroke timing.

Body position starts with hands and feet together

Pull, breathe, kick, glide sequence is performed

Swimmer returns to original body position.

Common Mistakes

As this stroke is a simultaneous stroke, it is very common to kick with the legs and pull with the arms at the same time. The result will be a very inefficient swimming stroke as the arms and legs counteract each other.

To ensure the timing and coordination of the arms and legs are correct, the swimmer must focus on performing an arm pull followed by a leg kick or on 'kicking their hands forwards'. In other words, as their legs kick around and back, their arms must extend forwards. This ensures that the arms and legs work efficiently and are extended out together during the glide phase.

Breaststroke Exercises

**'I hear and I forget
I see and I remember
I do and I understand'**
Confucius

Breaststroke Exercises

The lessons plans that follow on from these exercises cover lessons for beginners, intermediate and advanced swimmers. Although these exercises form the foundation from which to teach breaststroke, many other exercises are used throughout the lesson plans.

Every swimming teacher has their own 'take' on a particular exercise and many will have more exercises and drills in their repertoire to call upon. Listing all possible breaststroke exercises and drills and their variations would be an endless task and therefore beyond the scope of this book.

It is assumed that a swimming teacher will use their professional judgement and experience to make the best use of the exercises and lesson plans outlined here.

Body Position

Push and glide

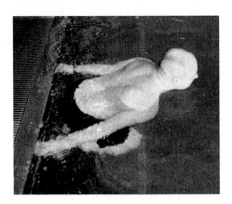 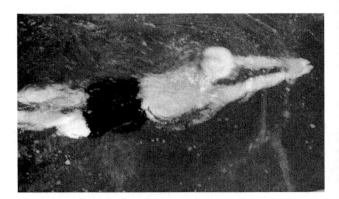

Aim: to develop a basic body position by pushing from the side.

The distance of the glide will be limited due to the resistance created by the chest and shoulders. The exercise can be performed with the face submerged as it would be during the glide phase of the stroke or with the head up facing forwards.

Teaching Points

- Push hard from the side
- Keep head up looking forward
- Stretch out as far as you can
- Keep your hands together
- Keep your feet together

Teacher's Focus

- Head remains still and central
- Face is up with only the chin in the water
- Eyes are looking forwards
- Shoulders are level and square
- Hips slightly below shoulder level
- Legs are in line with the body

Body Position
Push and glide

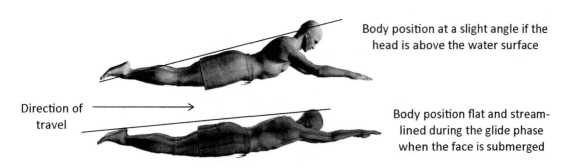

Body position at a slight angle if the head is above the water surface

Direction of travel

Body position flat and stream-lined during the glide phase when the face is submerged

Common Faults	Remedy
Shoulders and/or hips are not level	Reiterate the teaching point and repeat
Head is not central and still	Reiterate the teaching point and demonstrate
One shoulder is in front of the other	Encourage a straight and streamlined glide

Body Position

Static practice holding floats

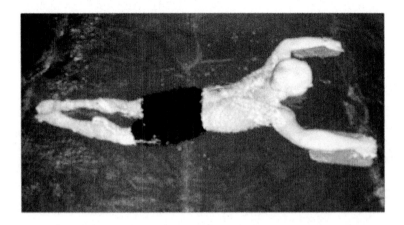

Aim: to help the swimmer develop confidence in their own buoyancy.

A float can be held under each arm or a single float held out in front, depending on levels of confidence and ability. Some swimmers may need extra assistance if they lack natural buoyancy.

Teaching Points

- Relax
- Keep the head tucked between the arms
- Stretch out as far as you can
- Keep your feet together

Teacher's Focus

- Head is central and still
- Face is submerged
- Eyes are looking downwards
- Shoulders should be level
- Hips are close to the surface
- Legs are together and in line with the body

Body Position
Static practice holding floats

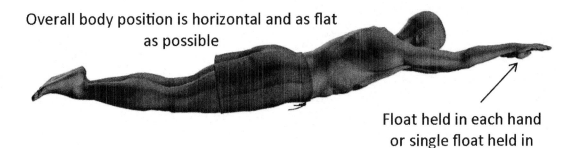

Overall body position is horizontal and as flat as possible

Float held in each hand or single float held in both hands

Common Faults	Remedy
Failure to submerge the face	Revert to previous exercises to build confidence
Head is not central	Reiterate the teaching point and demonstrate
Whole body is not remaining straight	Reiterate the teaching point and demonstrate
Feet and hands are not together	Reiterate the teaching point and demonstrate

Legs

Sitting on the poolside with feet in the water

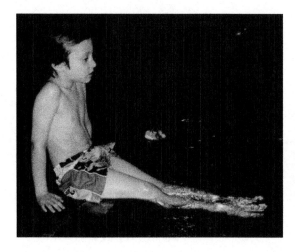 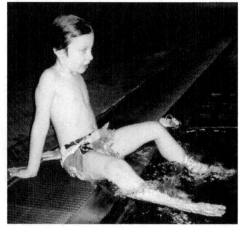

Aim: to practice the leg action whilst sat stationary on the poolside.

This exercise allows the pupil to copy the teacher who can also be sat on the poolside demonstrating the leg kick. The physical movement can be learnt before attempting the leg kick in the water.

Teaching Points

- Kick your legs simultaneously
- Keep your knees close together
- Kick like a frog
- Make sure your legs are straight and together at the end of the kick

Teacher's Focus

- Kick should be simultaneous
- Legs should be a mirror image
- Heels are drawn towards the seat
- The feet turn out just before the kick
- Feet come together at the end of the kick with legs straight and toes pointed

Sitting on the poolside with feet in the water

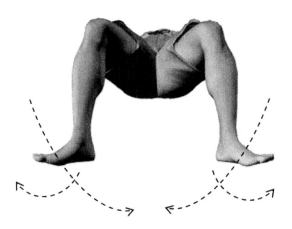

Feet turn out as the legs begin to kick round in a circular action

Common Faults	Remedy
Circular kick in the opposite direction	Demonstrate and repeat
Only turning one foot out	Reiterate the teaching point and demonstrate
Legs are not straight at the end of the kick	Reiterate the teaching point and demonstrate
Leg action is not circular	Demonstrate and assist as necessary

Legs

Supine position with a woggle held under the arms

Aim: to develop breaststroke leg kick in a supine position.

This allows the swimmer to see their own legs kicking. The woggle provides stability for the beginner and, with the swimmer in a supine position, allows the teacher easy communication during the exercise.

Teaching Points

- Kick with both legs at the same time
- Keep your feet in the water
- Kick like a frog
- Kick and glide
- Point your toes at the end of the kick

Teacher's Focus

- Kick should be simultaneous
- Heels are drawn towards the seat
- The feet turn out just before the kick
- Feet kick back with knees just inline with the hips
- Feet come together at the end of the kick

Push and glide from the side holding floats

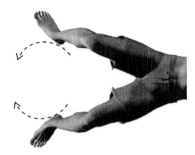

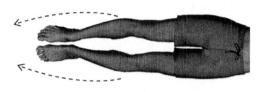

Heels drive back in a circular whip like action giving the kick power and motion

Kick finishes in a streamlined position with legs straight and toes pointed

Common Faults	Remedy
Feet are coming out of the water	Reiterate the teaching point and repeat
Failing to bring the heels up to the bottom	Repeat previous leg practice
Leg kick is not simultaneous	Reiterate teaching point and repeat
Legs are not straight at the end of the kick	Demonstrate and repeat

Legs

Static practice holding the poolside

Aim: to practise breaststroke leg action in a static position.

This allows the swimmer to develop correct technique in a prone position in the water. Kicking WITHOUT force and power should be encouraged during this exercise to avoid undue impact on the lower back.

Teaching Points

- Kick both legs at the same time
- Kick like a frog
- Draw a circle with your heels
- Make sure your legs are straight at the end of the kick

Teacher's Focus

- Legs should be a mirror image
- Heels are drawn towards the seat
- The feet turn out just before the kick
- Feet kick back with knees inline with the hips
- Feet come together at the end of the kick with legs straight and toes pointed

Legs
Static practice holding the poolside

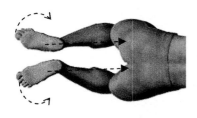

Heels drawn towards the seat and feet turn out

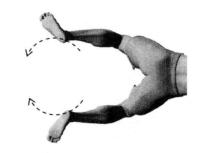

Heels draw round in a circular motion

Common Faults	Remedy
Only turning one foot out	Repeat previous leg practices
Legs are not simultaneous	Reiterate the teaching point
Leg action is not circular	Repeat previous leg practices

Legs

Prone position with a float held under each arm

Aim: to practise and develop correct leg technique in a prone position.

Using two floats aids balance and stability and encourages correct body position whilst moving through the water.

Teaching Points

- Keep your knees close together
- Point your toes to your shins
- Drive the water backwards with your heels
- Glide with legs straight at the end of the each kick

Teacher's Focus

- Leg kick should be simultaneous
- Heels are drawn towards the seat
- The feet turn out just before the kick
- Feet kick back with knees inline with the hips
- Feet come together at the end of the kick

Legs

Prone position with a float held under each arm

 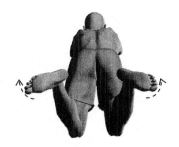 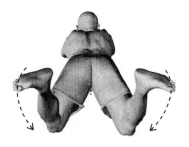

Heels are drawn up towards the seat. Soles face upwards

Feet turn outwards to allow the heels and soles to aid propulsion

Heels push back and outwards in a whip-like action

Common Faults	Remedy
One foot turns out, causing a 'scissor' like kick	Repeat earlier leg practices
Legs kick back and forth	Reiterate the teaching point, demonstrate and practice
Legs kick is not simultaneous	Reiterate the teaching point, demonstrate and practice
Toes are not pointed at the end of the kick	Reiterate the teaching point, demonstrate and practice

Legs

Holding a float out in front with both hands

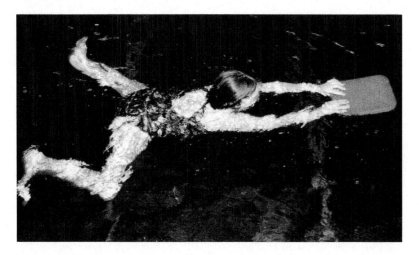

Aim: to practise and learn correct kicking technique and develop leg strength.

Holding a single float or kickboard out in front isolates the legs and creates a slight resistance which demands a stronger kick with which to maintain momentum.

Teaching Points

- Drive the water backwards with force
- Turn your feet out and drive the water with your heels
- Kick and glide
- Kick like a frog
- Make your feet like a penguin

Teacher's Focus

- Kick should be simultaneous
- Legs drive back to provide momentum
- Heels are drawn towards the seat
- The feet turn out before the kick
- Feet come together at the end of the kick with legs straight and toes pointed

Legs
Holding a float out in front with both hands

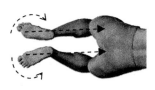 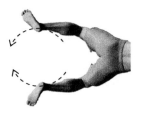 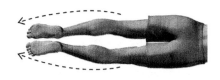

Heels drawn towards the seat and feet turn out

Heels drive back in a circular whip like action giving the kick power and motion

Kick finishes in a streamlined position with legs straight and toes pointed

Common Faults	Remedy
Kick is slow and lacking power	Repeat earlier leg practices
Failing to bring the heels up to the bottom	Repeat earlier leg practices
Feet are breaking the water surface	Check the body position and correct
Toes are not pointed at the end of the kick	Reiterate the teaching point and repeat

Legs

Holding a float vertically in front

Aim: to learn correct kicking technique and develop leg strength.

The float held vertically adds resistance to the movement and requires the swimmer to kick with greater effort. Ideal for swimmers with a weak leg kick.

Teaching Points

- Kick your legs simultaneously
- Push the water with your heels and the soles of your feet
- Drive the water backwards with your heels

Teacher's Focus

- Arms should be straight and float held partly underwater
- Kick should be a whip like action
- Feet kick back with knees inline with the hips
- Feet come together at the end of the kick
- Upper body and arms should be relaxed

Legs
Holding a float vertically in front

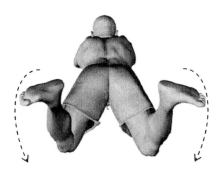

Heels push back and outwards in a whip-like action

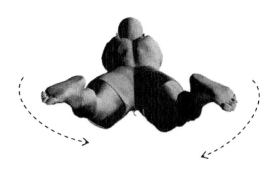

Heels drive back to add power to the kick

Common Faults	Remedy
Float is held flat or out of the water	Demonstrate and repeat
Not turning both feet out	Reiterate the teaching point or revert back to a previous exercise
Leg kick lacks sufficient power	Reiterate the teaching point or revert back to a previous exercise

51

Legs

Supine position with hands held on hips

Aim: to practise and learn correct kicking technique.

This exercise is more advanced and requires the leg kick to be previously well practised.

Teaching Points

- Keep your feet in the water
- Kick like a frog
- Make sure your legs are straight after each kick
- Kick and glide
- Point your toes at the end of the kick

Teacher's Focus

- Kick should be simultaneous
- Heels are drawn towards the seat
- The feet turn out just before the kick
- Feet kick back with knees inline with the hips
- Feet come together at the end of the kick with legs straight and toes pointed

Legs

Supine position with hands held on hips

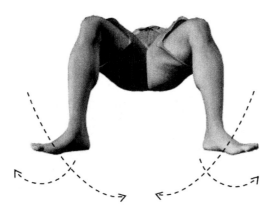

Feet turn out as the legs begin to kick round in a circular action

Common Faults	Remedy
Not turning both feet out	Reiterate the teaching point, demonstrate and practice
Kick is not hard enough to provide power	Repeat the previous leg practice
Legs are not straight at the end of the kick	Reiterate the teaching point, demonstrate and practice
Toes are not pointed at the end of the kick	Reiterate the teaching point, demonstrate and practice

Legs

Moving practice with arms stretched out in front

Aim: to practise correct kicking technique and develop leg strength.

This is an advanced exercise as holding the arms out in front demands a stronger kick with which to maintain momentum whilst maintaining a streamlined body position.

Teaching Points

- Keep your knees close together
- Drive the water with your heels
- Make sure your legs are straight at the end of the kick
- Kick and glide

Teacher's Focus

- Kick should be simultaneous
- The feet turn out just before the kick
- Feet kick back with knees just inline with the hips
- Feet come together at the end of the kick with legs straight and toes pointed

Legs
Moving practice with arms stretched out in front

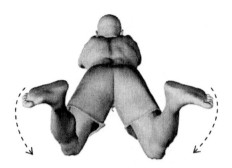

Heels push back and outwards in a
whip-like action

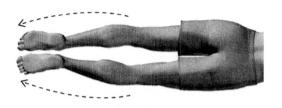

Kick finishes in a streamlined position
with legs straight and toes pointed

Common Faults	Remedy
Not turning both feet out	Reiterate the teaching point, demonstrate and practice
Feet are breaking the water surface	Check the body position or revert to earlier exercises
Legs are not straight at the end of the kick	Revert to earlier leg kick practices
Toes are not pointed at the end of the kick	Revert to earlier leg kick practices

Arms

Static practice standing on the poolside

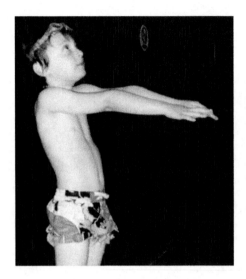 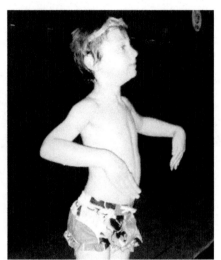

Aim: to learn the arm pull technique in its most basic form.

On the poolside, either sitting or standing, the swimmer can practise and perfect the movement without the resistance of the water.

Teacher's Focus

- Both arms pull at the same time
- Keep your fingers closed together
- Keep your hands flat
- Tuck your elbows into your sides after each pull
- Stretch your arms forward until they are straight
- Draw an upside down heart with your hands

Teaching Points

- Arm action should be simultaneous
- Fingers should be together
- Arm pull should be circular
- Elbows should be tucked in after each pull
- Arms should extend forward and together after each pull

Static practice standing on the poolside

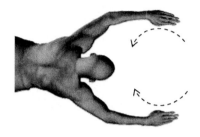

Arms and hands pull around and downwards

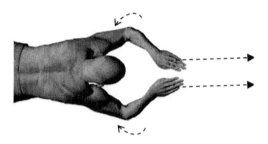

Elbows tuck in and arms extend forward

Common Faults	Remedy
Fingers apart	Reiterate the teaching point, demonstrate and practice
Arms pull at different speeds	Demonstrate and repeat
Arms pull past the shoulders	Demonstrate and repeat
Elbows fail to tuck in each time	Reiterate the teaching point, demonstrate and practice
Arms fail to extend full forward	Demonstrate and repeat

Arms

Walking practice moving through shallow water

Aim: to practise and develop correct arm technique from in the water.

The swimmer can experience the feel of pulling the water whilst walking along the pool floor. Where the water is too deep, this exercise can be performed standing on the poolside. Submerging the face is optional at this stage.

Teaching Points

- Pull with both arms at the same time
- Keep your hands under the water
- Tuck your elbows into your sides after each pull
- Stretch your arms forward until they are straight
- Draw an upside down heart with your hands

Teacher's Focus

- Arm action should be simultaneous
- Arms and hands should remain under water
- Fingers should be together
- Arms should extend forward and together until straight after each pull

Arms
Walking practice moving through shallow water

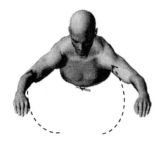

Arms and hands pull back in a
circular motion

Elbows tuck in and arms and hands stretch
forward into a glide

Common Faults	Remedy
Fingers are too wide apart	Reiterate the teaching point, demonstrate and practice
Arms pull past the shoulders	Demonstrate and repeat
Elbows fail to tuck in each time	Demonstrate and repeat
Arms fail to extend full forward	Reiterate the teaching point, demonstrate and practice
Hands come out of the water	Reiterate the teaching point, demonstrate and practice

Arms

Moving practice with a woggle held under the arms

Aim: to learn correct arm action whilst moving through the water.

The use of the woggle means that leg kicks are not required to assist motion and this then helps develop strength in the arm pull. The woggle slightly restricts arm action but not enough to negate the benefits of this exercise.

Teaching Points

- Pull round in a circle
- Keep your hands under the water
- Keep your fingers together and hands flat
- Pull your body through the water
- Draw an upside down heart with your hands

Teacher's Focus

- Arm action should be simultaneous
- Arms and hands should remain under water
- Arms and hands should extend forward after the pull
- Fingers should be together
- Arm pull should be circular

Arms

Moving practice with a woggle held under the arms

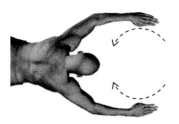 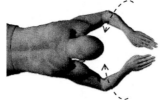 

Arms and hands pull around and downwards

Elbows tuck in and arms and hands stretch forward into a glide

Common Faults	Remedy
Fingers are too wide apart	Repeat earlier arm practices
Arms fail to extend fully forward	Demonstrate and repeat
Hands come out of the water	Reiterate the teaching point and repeat
Arms extend forward too far apart	Reiterate the teaching point and repeat

Arms

Arms only with a pull-buoy held between the legs

Aim: to develop strength in the arm pull.

The pull-buoy prevents the legs from kicking, therefore isolating the arms. As the legs are stationary, forward propulsion and a glide action is difficult and therefore the arm action is made stronger as it has to provide all the propulsion for this exercise.

Teaching Points

- Keep your hands under the water
- Pull your body through the water
- Keep your elbows high as you pull
- Tuck your elbows into your sides after each pull
- Stretch your arms forward until they are straight

Teacher's Focus

- Arms and hands should remain under water
- Arm pull should be circular
- Elbows should be tucked in after each pull
- Arms should extend forward and together

Arms

Alternating arm pull whilst holding a float out in front

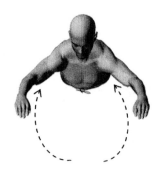

Arms and hands pull back in a
circular motion

Elbows tuck in and arms and hands
stretch forward together

Common Faults	Remedy
Arms pull past the shoulders	Reiterate the teaching point, demonstrate and practice
Elbows fail to tuck in each time	Revert to the previous arm practice
Arms fail to extend full forward	Reiterate the teaching point, demonstrate and practice
Hands come out of the water	Revert to the previous arm practice
Arms extend forward too far apart	Reiterate the teaching point, demonstrate and practice

Arms

Push and glide adding arm pulls

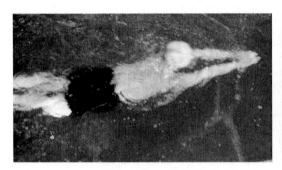 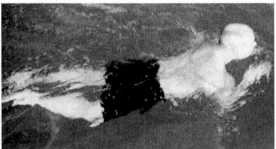

Aim: to progress arm action and technique from previous exercises.

By incorporating a push and glide, this allows the swimmer to practise maintaining a correct body position whilst using the arms. This is a more advanced exercise as the number of arms pulls and distance travelled will vary according to the strength of the swimmer.

Teaching Points

- Keep your hands under the water
- Pull your body through the water
- Tuck your elbows into your sides after each pull
- Stretch your arms forward with hands together

Teacher's Focus

- Arms and hands should remain under water
- Elbows should be tucked in after each pull
- Arms should extend forward into a glide position
- Body position should be maintained throughout

Arms
Push and glide adding arm pulls

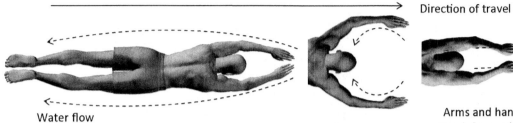

Direction of travel

Water flow

Arms and hands pull around
and downwards

Arms and hands
stretch forward into
the original glide
position

Common Faults	Remedy
Arms pull past the shoulders	Revert to the previous arm practice
Arms fail to extend full forward	Reiterate the teaching point, demonstrate and practice
Hands come out of the water	Repeat earlier arm practices
Arms extend forward too far apart	Reiterate the teaching point and repeat
Arms fail to bend during the pull	Repeat earlier arm practices

Breathing

Static practice, breathing with arm action

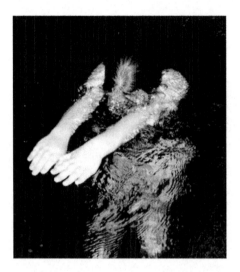 

Aim: to practise breaststroke breathing action whilst standing in the water.

This allows the swimmer to experience the feel of breathing into the water in time with the arm action, without the need to actually swim.

Teaching Points

- Breathe in as you complete your arm pull
- Breathe out as your hands stretch forwards
- Blow your hands forwards

Teacher's Focus

- Breath inwards at the end of the in sweep
- Head lifts up as the arms complete the pull
- Head should clear the water
- Head returns to the water as the arms recover
- Breath out is as the hands recover forward

Breathing

Push and glide adding arm cycles

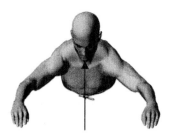

Breathe IN as the arms pull
down and the head rises

Breathe OUT as the arms recover
forward and the face enters the
water

Common Faults	Remedy
Head fails to clear the water	Reiterate the teaching point, demonstrate and practice
Breathing out as the arms pull back	Reiterate the teaching point, demonstrate and practice
Lifting the head to breathe as the arms recover	Reiterate the teaching point, demonstrate and practice

Breathing

Breathing practice with woggle under the arms

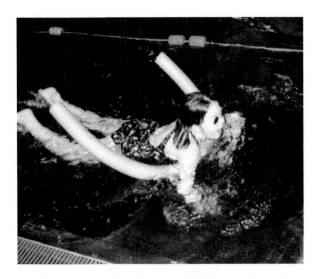

Aim: to develop correct synchronisation of breathing and arm pull technique.

The woggle provides support, which enables the exercise to be done slowly at first. It also allows the swimmer to travel during the practice. Leg action can be added if necessary. Note: the woggle can restrict complete arm action.

Teaching Points

- Breathe in as you complete your arm pull
- Breathe out as your hands stretch forwards
- Blow your hands forwards

Teacher's Focus

- Breath inwards at the end of the in-sweep
- Head lifts up as the arms complete the pull back
- Head should clear the water
- Head returns to the water as the arms recover
- Breathing out is as the hands stretch forward

Breathing
Breathing practice with woggle under the arms

Breathe IN

Breathing in occurs as the arms pull down and the head rises above the surface

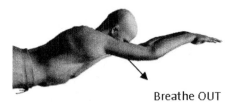

Breathe OUT

Breathing out occurs as the arms recover out in front

Common Faults	Remedy
Holding the breath	Revert to previous basic breathing exercises to encourage breathing out
Head fails to clear the water	Revert to previous basic breathing exercises to encourage breathing out
Breathing out as the arms pull back	Revert to previous basic breathing exercises to encourage breathing out
Lifting the head as the arms stretch forward	Reiterate the teaching point, demonstrate and practice

Breathing

Float held in front, breathing with leg kick

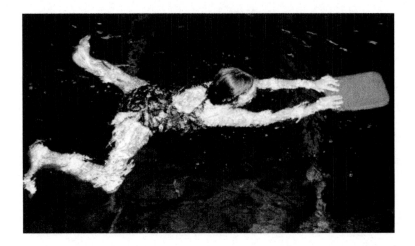

Aim: to develop the breathing technique in time with the leg kick.

The float provides stability and allows the swimmer to focus on the breathe kick glide action.

Teaching Points

- Breathe in as your legs bend ready to kick
- Breathe out as you kick and glide
- Kick your head down

Teacher's Focus

- Inward breathing should be just before the knees bend
- Head lifts up as the knees bend ready to kick
- Mouth should clear the water
- Head returns to the water as the legs thrust backwards
- Breathe out is as the legs kick into a glide

Breathing
Float held in front, breathing with leg kick

Breathe IN just before the knees bend for the kick

Breathe OUT as the legs kick into a glide

Common Faults	Remedy
Holding the breath	Revert to previous basic breathing exercises to encourage breathing out
Head fails to clear the water	Revert to earlier breathing practices
Breathing out as the knees bend ready to kick	Reiterate the teaching point and repeat
Lifting the head as the legs kick into a glide	Reiterate the teaching point and repeat

Timing

Slow practice with woggle under the arms

Aim: to practise the stroke timing in its most basic form.

The use of the woggle placed under the arms allows the swimmer to practice the exercise in stages as slowly as they need. It must be noted that the woggle resists against the glide and therefore the emphasis must be placed on the timing of the arms and legs. The glide can be developed using other exercises.

Teaching Points

- Pull with your hands first
- Kick your hands forwards
- Kick your body into a glide
- Pull, breathe, kick, glide

Teacher's Focus

- From a streamlined position arms should pull first
- Legs should kick into a glide
- Legs should kick as the hands and arms recover
- A glide should precede the next arm pull

Timing

Slow practice with woggle under the arms

Body position starts with hands and feet together

Pull, breathe, kick, glide sequence is performed

Swimmer returns to original body position.

Common Faults	Remedy
Kicking and pulling at the same time	Reiterate the teaching point, demonstrate and practice
Failure to glide	Reiterate the teaching point, demonstrate and practice
Legs kick whilst gliding	Reiterate the teaching point, demonstrate and practice

Timing

Push and glide, adding stroke cycles

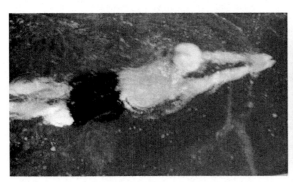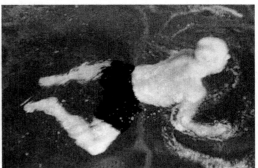

Aim: to practise and develop correct stroke timing.

The swimmer starts with a push and glide to establish a streamlined glide. The arm pull, breath in and then leg kick is executed in the correct sequence, resulting in another streamlined glide.

Teaching Points

- Kick your hands forwards
- Kick your body into a glide
- Pull, breathe, kick, glide

Teacher's Focus

- From a streamlined position arms should pull first
- Legs should kick into a glide
- Legs should kick as the hands and arms recover
- A glide should precede the next arm pull

Timing

Push and glide, adding stroke cycles

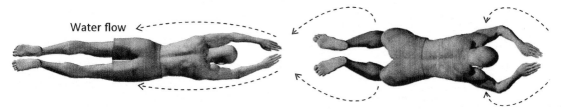

Water flow

Push and glide to establish body position

Pull, breathe, kick and glide again

Common Faults	Remedy
Kicking and pulling at the same time	Repeat previous timing practice
Failure to glide	Reiterate the teaching point and repeat
Legs kick whilst gliding	Reiterate the teaching point and repeat

Timing

Two kicks, one arm pull

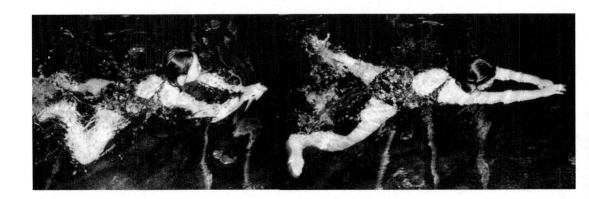

Aim: to perfect timing whilst maintaining a streamlined body position.

From a push and glide, the swimmer performs a 'pull, breathe, kick, glide' stroke cycle into another streamlined glide. They then perform an additional kick whilst keeping the hands and arms stretched out in front. This encourages concentration on timing and coordination and at the same time develops leg kick strength.

Teaching Points

- Kick your body into a glide
- Pull, breathe, kick, glide

Teacher's Focus

- Legs should kick into a glide
- Legs should kick as the hands and arms recover
- A glide should follow each leg kick
- Head lifts to breath with each arm pull

Timing
Two kicks, one arm pull

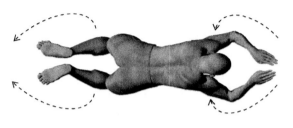

A full stroke cycle is performed
from a push and glide

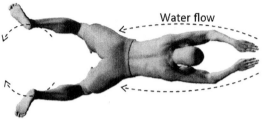

Water flow

Additional kick whilst the hands and
arms remain still

Common Faults	Remedy
Arms pull too often and too early	Reiterate the teaching point, demonstrate and practice
Failure to glide	Repeat earlier timing practices
Failure to keep the hands together for the second kick	Reiterate the teaching point, demonstrate and practice

Full Stroke

Aim: to swim full stroke Breast Stroke demonstrating efficient arm and leg action, with regular breathing and correct timing.

Teaching Points

- Kick and glide
- Kick your hands forwards
- Drive your feet backward through the water
- Keep your fingers together and under the water
- Pull in a small circle then stretch forward
- Breath with each stroke

Teacher's Focus

- Head remains still and central
- Shoulders remain level
- Leg kick is simultaneous
- Feet turn out and drive backwards
- Arm action should be circular and simultaneous
- Breathing is regular with each stroke cycle

Common Faults	Remedy
Failure to glide	Repeat earlier timing practices
Stroke is rushed	Encourage a longer glide and repeat
Leg kick is not simultaneous	Repeat earlier leg practices
Arms pull to the sides	Repeat earlier arm practices
Failing to breath regularly	Repeat earlier breathing practices

Lesson Plans

Lesson Plan Layout

Lesson Plan #2

Lesson type: full stroke front crawl
Level: adult or child intermediate
Previous learning: basic front crawl technique
Lesson aim: to progress and develop the whole stroke
Equipment: floats, pull buoys, sinkers and hoop

Lesson type: the part of breaststroke that this lesson focuses on. For example, **Breaststroke Leg Kick**.

Level: who the lesson is aimed at if they are beginners, intermediate or advanced level. For example, **Child Beginner.**

Previous learning: the aspects of swimming the pupil is expected to have covered before this lesson. For example, **basic front paddle**. The pupil is *not* expected to have completely mastered an aspect of swimming but should have had some experience of learning it.

Lesson aim: the lesson objective or desired outcome of the lesson. For example, **'to learn basic breaststroke leg kick and introduce breathing'**.

Equipment: the equipment you will need for this lesson. For example, **'floats, buoyancy aids and hoop'**.

Lesson Sequences

Lesson plans are laid out in a sequence (beginner, intermediate, advanced) to give the teacher easy reference to other lessons, exercises, and activities. This layout should allow for easier differentiation across varying abilities.

Lesson plans do not have to be followed in sequence, although they can be if you wish. Each plan has its aim and therefore can be used in sequence with other lessons aimed at that level to suit the individual pupil or pupils.

These lesson plans and the exercises and activities are set out as a guide. Every pupil is different and will interpret and respond to practices and teaching points in their way, therefore as a swimming teacher; it is essential to be flexible in your approach. In other words, where a pupil finds a particular exercise difficult, choose an easier exercise from a previous plan. Where a pupil is not quite grasping the concept of what you are teaching, try using a different phrase or teaching point.

Teaching Points

Teaching points are our 'magic words'. Having various teaching points in our virtual tool kit can be extremely useful. For example, when you say to a pupil 'turn our feet out, and they just don't get it, you change the teaching point to 'turn your toes up as you kick around'. Suddenly, they are kicking with their feet in the right position.

Learning to be creative with our teaching points can be a very powerful skill and can be the difference between a pupil struggling and that light bulb moment when they suddenly understand and can do it.

Organising Your Swimmers

The way you choose to organise your swimmers as they swim off to perform a given exercise is vital to maintaining a safe learning environment and monitoring their progress.

The organisation column of the lesson plans makes a suggestion. Still, you will have to use your professional judgement based on the size of your class and the swimming lesson area available in your pool.

The suggestions are:

All together - you instruct all swimmers to go at the same time. Ideal if you have sufficient space and can be unsafe if you do not.

Waves - number your swimmers 1 and 2 alternately (or more if you have a large class). Then instruct all numbers 1's to go first, followed by the number 2's and so on, if you have more. This method of organisation is a good way of monitoring swimmers and a great way to organise large classes of advanced swimmers.

One-by-one - sending each swimmer off one at a time is an ideal method for monitoring each pupil closely.

Getting The Timing Right

All swimming pools vary in their dimensions, and often larger pools have an area roped off for swimming lessons, so the whole pool is rarely used. These plans assume that beginner and intermediate swimmers will swim widths and advanced swimmers will swim lengths. The size of the width and length in *your* pool might not fit in with how these plans are formatted, and you may wish to use your professional judgment to change them to suit your circumstances.

The duration of most swimming lessons is about 30 minutes. The timings of each exercise in these lesson plans are a guide and again, your professional judgement can be used to adjust them to suit your pupils and your pool size.

If you begin to discover that you are racing through the lesson and will have time left over, remember any exercise can be repeated. Repeating an exercise will enhance a pupil's strength, stamina and overall ability. A different teaching point can also be used to help those that perhaps did not quite get it the first time around.

Important Terminology:

Prone - 'facing downwards'. For example, a prone push and glide is performed in the face-down position.

Supine - 'facing downwards' For example, a supine star float is performed on the back, facing upwards.

'By failing to prepare
you are preparing to fail.'
Benjamin Franklin

Lesson Plan #1

Lesson type: full stroke breaststroke
Level: adult or child beginner
Previous learning: Child - basic front paddle Adult - none
Lesson aim: to learn the basics of breaststroke and experience the whole stroke
Equipment: floats, woggle, buoyancy aids if needed and hoop

Exercise/Activity	Teaching Points	Organisation	Duration
Entry: swivel or steps entry	enter slowly	all together	1 min
Warm up: 2 widths any stroke with buoyancy aids if needed	take your time	all together	3 mins
Main Theme: full stroke, slowly with a woggle under the arms	pull in a circle, kick in a circle	all together	2 mins
push and glide, holding floats if needed	stretch out and relax	waves	3 mins
supine kicking with woggle under arms	turn out your feet	waves	3 mins
arm pulls, walking through shallow water	keep hands underwater	waves	4 mins
arm pulls with breathing, woggle under the arms	blow your hands forwards	waves	3 mins
full stroke, with bouyancy aids if needed	pull *then* kick	waves	3 mins
Contrasting Activity: supine star float	stretch out and relax	2 or 3 at a time	3 mins
sitting dive through a hoop at the surface	head tucked down	2 or 3 at a time	3 mins
Exit: using the pool steps or over the poolside	take your time	one by one	1 min

Total time: 29 minutes

Lesson #1 Assessment

Lesson Objective: to learn each part of basic breaststroke and experience the whole stroke.

Below average	Average	Above average
😐	🙂	😎
Attempts to demonstrate but does not show the correct technique	Able to perform most of the technique correctly some of the time	Performs the technique correctly most of the time

Assessment	😐	🙂	😎
Arms pull in a circular path			
Legs kick in a circular path			
Feet attempt to turn outwards			
Exhalation takes place underwater			
Arm pull and leg kick sequence is continuous			

Lesson Plan #2

Lesson type: full stroke breaststroke
Level: adult or child intermediate
Previous learning: basic breaststroke technique
Lesson aim: to progress and develop the whole stroke to an intermediate level
Equipment: floats, sinkers and hoop

Exercise/Activity	Teaching Points	Organisation	Duration
Entry: swivel or sitting dive entry	enter slowly	waves	1 min
Warm up: 2 widths any stroke	take your time	all together	3 mins
Main Theme: 2 widths full stroke breaststroke with buoyancy aids if needed	pull in a circle, kick in a circle	waves	2 mins
push and glide from the poolside	hands and feet together	one by one	3 mins
kicking with a float under each arm	knees together and kick around	waves	3 mins
push and glide adding arm pulls	pull in small circles	waves	3 mins
kicking with a float, adding breathing	kick and blow out	waves	3 mins
full stroke without buoyancy aids	kick your hands forwards	waves	3 mins
Contrasting Activity: head first surface dives, collecting sinkers placed apart	deep breath and dig down	one by one	3 mins
dolphin kick through a hoop at the surface	swim like a mermaid	one by one	3 mins
Exit: using the pool steps or over the poolside	take your time	one by one	1 min

Total time: 28 minutes

Lesson #2 Assessment

Lesson Objective: to progress and develop the whole stroke to an intermediate level.

Below average	Average	Above average
😐	🙂	😎
Attempts to demonstrate but does not show the correct technique	Able to perform most of the technique correctly some of the time	Performs the technique correctly most of the time

Assessment	😐	🙂	😎
Arms pull in a small circle			
Legs kick in a circular path with knees close together			
Feet attempt to turn outwards			
Exhalation takes place as the legs kick around and back			
Arms pull and legs kick in an alternating sequence.			

Lesson Plan #3

Lesson type: full stroke breaststroke

Level: adult or child advanced
Previous learning: full stroke breaststroke
Lesson aim: to develop and fine-tune technique for the whole stroke
Equipment: floats

Exercise/Activity	Teaching Points	Organisation	Duration
Entry: sitting or shallow dive entry	take your time	waves	1 min
Warm up: 2 lengths any stroke	take your time	all together	3 mins
Main Theme: 2 lengths full stroke breaststroke	stretch and glide	waves	2 mins
kicking with a float held vertically	feet whip around with power	waves	3 mins
push and glide, adding arm pull into another glide	hands stay in front of shoulders	waves	3 mins
full stroke breathing alternate stroke cycles	blow your hands forwards	waves	3 mins
full stroke, 2 legs kicks to 1 arm pull	kick and glide	waves	3 mins
2 lengths full stroke breaststroke	smooth flowing movements	waves	3 mins
Contrasting Activity: dolphin kick underwater, arms by sides	lead with your head	one by one	3 mins
treading water	head above the water	waves	3 mins
Exit: using the pool steps or over the poolside	take your time	one by one	1 min

Total time: 28 minutes

Lesson #3 Assessment

Lesson Objective: to develop and fine-tune technique for the whole stroke.		
Below average	**Average**	**Above average**
😐	🙂	😎
Attempts to demonstrate but does not show the correct technique	**Able to perform most of the technique correctly some of the time**	**Performs the technique correctly most of the time**

Assessment	😐	🙂	😎
Arms pull in a small circle and elbows tuck in			
Legs kick in a powerful whips action with knees close together			
Feet turn out to kick and then point to glide			
Inhalation takes place as the arms pull			
Exhalation takes place as the legs kick into a glide			
pull, breathe, kick, glide' sequence is smooth and continuous			

Lesson Plan #4

Lesson type: breaststroke body position
Level: adult or child beginner
Previous learning: basic front paddle and submerging the face
Lesson aim: to learn basic breaststroke body position
Equipment: floats, woggles and sinkers

Exercise/Activity	Teaching Points	Organisation	Duration
Entry: swivel entry	enter slowly	all together	1 min
Warm up: 2 widths any stroke using buoyancy aids	take your time	all together	3 mins
Main Theme: floating holding the poolside, using buoyancy aids if needed	feel the water supporting you	all together	2 mins
floating with float held under each arm	lay flat and streamlined	all together	2 mins
push and glide with a float under each arm	face in the water	waves	4 mins
push and glide with a woggle to support	face in the water and stretch out	waves	3 mins
push and glide with arms extended	hands and feet together	waves	2 mins
full stroke breaststroke with buoyancy aids if needed	pull and kick in a circle	waves	3 mins
Contrasting Activity: submerging to collect an object	take your time	2 or 3 at a time	4 mins
tuck (mushroom) float	chin and knees to chest	all together	2 mins
Exit: using the pool steps or over the poolside	take your time	one by one	1 min

Total time: 27 minutes

Lesson #4 Assessment

Lesson Objective: to learn basic breaststroke body position.		
Below average	**Average**	**Above average**
😐	🙂	😎
Attempts to demonstrate but does not show the correct technique	Able to perform most of the technique correctly some of the time	Performs the technique correctly most of the time

Assessment	😐	🙂	😎
Face is submerged			
Body position is flat			
Legs and feet are together			
Hands are together			
Hips are level			
Shoulders are level			

Lesson Plan #5

Lesson type: breaststroke body position
Level: adult or child intermediate
Previous learning: basic breaststroke breaststroke technique
Lesson aim: to improve basic breaststroke body position and shape
Equipment: floats and/or woggles and hoop

Exercise/Activity	Teaching Points	Organisation	Duration
Entry: swivel entry	enter slowly	all together	1 min
Warm up: 2 widths any stroke without using buoyancy aids	take your time	all together	3 mins
Main Theme: push and glide using buoyancy aids if needed	relax and stretch	waves	3 mins
push and glide without buoyancy aids	arm extended with face submerged	waves	3 mins
push and glide adding leg kicks, returning to a glide position	feet together when gliding	waves	3 mins
push and glide adding arm pull, returning to a glide position	hands together when gliding	waves	3 mins
push and glide adding 1 arm pull, 1 leg kick and return to glide	hands and feet together to glide	waves	3 mins
2 widths full stroke breaststroke	pull, kick and then glide	waves	3 mins
Contrasting Activity: forward somersault from a push and glide	tuck chin on chest	2 or 3 at a time	3 mins
sitting dive through a submerged hoop	hands together	2 or 3 at a time	3 mins
Exit: using the pool steps or over the poolside	take your time	one by one	1 min

Total time: 29 minutes

Lesson #5 Assessment

Lesson Objective: to improve basic breaststroke body position and shape.		
Below average	**Average**	**Above average**
🙂	🙂	😎
Attempts to demonstrate but does not show the correct technique	**Able to perform most of the technique correctly some of the time**	**Performs the technique correctly most of the time**

Assessment	🙂	🙂	😎
Face is submerged whilst moving			
Body position is horizontal			
Feet are together whilst gliding			
Hands are together whilst gliding			
Hips remain level whilst gliding			
Shoulders remain level whilst gliding			

Lesson Plan #6

Lesson type: breaststroke body position
Level: adult or child advanced
Previous learning: full stroke breaststroke
Lesson aim: to develop and fine-tune breaststroke body position and shape
Equipment: buoyancy aids if needed

Exercise/Activity	Teaching Points	Organisation	Duration
Entry: sitting or shallow dive entry	take your time	all together	1 min
Warm up: 2 lengths any stroke	steady pace	all together	3 mins
Main Theme: 2 lengths full stroke breaststroke	let the stroke flow	all together	3 mins
push and glide with face submerged	cut through the water	waves	3 mins
push and glide adding leg kicks, counting a 2 second glide between kicks	feet together when gliding	waves	3 mins
push and glide adding arm pulls, counting a 2 second glide between pulls	hands together when gliding	waves	3 mins
full stroke with 2 legs kicks to 1 arm pull	streamlined shape when gliding	waves	3 mins
2 lengths full stroke breaststroke	pull, kick and glide	waves	3 mins
Contrasting Activity: supine push and glide and rotate to prone position	keep head level	2 or 3 at a time	3 mins
any stroke with somersault mid swim	head down, chin to chest	2 or 3 at a time	3 mins
Exit: using the pool steps or over the poolside	take your time	all together	1 min

Total time: 29 minutes

Lesson #6 Assessment

Lesson Objective: to develop and fine-tune breaststroke body position and shape.	

Below average	Average	Above average
😐	🙂	😎
Attempts to demonstrate but does not show the correct technique	**Able to perform most of the technique correctly some of the time**	**Performs the technique correctly most of the time**

Assessment	😐	🙂	😎
Face is submerged and head is level			
Body position remains streamlined whilst gliding			
Feet are together with toes pointed whilst gliding			
Arms are stretched out and streamlined			
Hips and shoulders are level whilst gliding			
Head remains in a neutral position whilst gliding			

Lesson Plan #7

Lesson type: breaststroke leg kick
Level: adult or child beginner
Previous learning: basic front paddle and gliding
Lesson aim: to learn basic breaststroke leg kick
Equipment: floats or kick-boards, buoyancy aids as necessary and hoop

Exercise/Activity	Teaching Points	Organisation	Duration
Entry: swivel entry	enter slowly	all together	1 min
Warm up: 2 widths any stroke using buoyancy aids	take your time	all together	3 mins
Main Theme: sitting the poolside demonstrating kicking action	Diamond, star, crocodile snap!	all together	2 mins
full stroke with buoyancy aids	kick like a frog	all together	3 mins
kicking with a float held under each arm	kick around and together	waves	3 mins
kicking supine with a float held under each arm	turn out your feet like a penguin	waves	4 mins
kicking with one float held in front	kick and glide	waves	3 mins
full stroke with buoyancy aids if necessary	breathe, kick, glide	all together	3 mins
Contrasting Activity: supine star float	chin to chest	one by one	2 mins
push and glide through a hoop	hands and feet together	one by one	2 mins
Exit: using the pool steps	take your time	one by one	1 min

Total time: 27 minutes

Lesson #7 Assessment

Lesson Objective: to learn basic breaststroke leg kick and introduce breathing.		
Below average	**Average**	**Above average**
😐	🙂	😎
Attempts to demonstrate but does not show the correct technique	Able to perform most of the technique correctly some of the time	Performs the technique correctly most of the time

Assessment	😐	🙂	😎
Legs kick simultaneously in a circular path			
Feet turn outwards			
Feet return together			
Kick is followed by a glide			

Lesson Plan #8

Lesson type: breaststroke leg kick
Level: adult or child intermediate
Previous learning: basic breaststroke technique
Lesson aim: to strengthen and develop basic breaststroke leg kick
Equipment: floats, buoyancy aids and hoop

Exercise/Activity	Teaching Points	Organisation	Duration
Entry: swivel or sitting dive entry	enter slowly	all together	1 min
Warm up: 2 widths full stroke breaststroke	take your time	all together	3 mins
Main Theme: supine leg kick with woggle or floats	kick and glide	all together	2 mins
kicking with a float held under each arm	snap feet together	waves	3 mins
kicking with one float held in front	kick with power	waves	3 mins
kicking with one float held in front adding a glide	feet together when gliding	waves	3 mins
kick with floats held under each arm plus breaths	kick and blow	waves	3 mins
2 widths full stroke breaststroke	breathe, kick, glide	all together	3 mins
Contrasting Activity: sitting dives	chin to chest	one by one	3 mins
push and glide through a submerged hoop	hands and feet together	one by one	3 mins
Exit: using the pool steps	take your time	one by one	1 min

Total time: 28 minutes

Lesson #8 Assessment

Lesson Objective: to strengthen and develop basic breaststroke leg kick.		
Below average	**Average**	**Above average**
😐	🙂	😎
Attempts to demonstrate but does not show the correct technique	Able to perform most of the technique correctly some of the time	Performs the technique correctly most of the time

Assessment	😐	🙂	😎
Legs kick simultaneously with power			
Feet turn outwards			
Feet return together with toes pointed			
Kick is followed by a streamlined glide			

Lesson Plan #9

Lesson type: breaststroke leg kick
Level: adult or child advanced
Previous learning: full stroke breaststroke
Lesson aim: to develop and perfect breaststroke leg kick
Equipment: floats or kickboards

Exercise/Activity	Teaching Points	Organisation	Duration
Entry: sitting or shallow dive entry	take your time	waves	1 min
Warm up: 2 lengths any stroke	take your time	all together	3 mins
Main Theme: 2 lengths full stroke breaststroke	smooth flowing movements	all together	3 mins
leg kicks with a float held vertically	whip your feet around	waves	3 mins
kicking with a float held in front, counting leg kicks	kick and glide	one by one	3 mins
kicking with arms extended, counting leg kicks	feet whip together	waves	3 mins
kicking vertically (treading water) in deep water	push with your heels	all together	3 mins
2 lengths full stroke breaststroke	kick into a glide	all together	3 mins
Contrasting Activity: push and glide into forward somersault	arms pull down to rotate	2 or 3 at a time	2 mins
supine push and glide into somersault	tuck chin to chest	2 or 3 at a time	2 mins
Exit: using the pool steps	take your time	waves	1 min

Total time: 27 minutes

Lesson #9 Assessment

Lesson Objective: to develop and perfect breaststroke leg kick.		
Below average	**Average**	**Above average**
😐	🙂	😎
Attempts to demonstrate but does not show the correct technique	Able to perform most of the technique correctly some of the time	Performs the technique correctly most of the time

Assessment	😐	🙂	😎
Legs kick simultaneously with power			
Feet turn outwards and then whip around			
Feet return together with toes pointed			
Kick is followed by a streamlined glide			

Lesson Plan #10

Lesson type: breaststroke arms
Level: adult or child beginner
Previous learning: basic breaststroke technique
Lesson aim: to learn and practice basic breaststroke arm pull
Equipment: floats, buoyancy aids as necessary and hoop

Exercise/Activity	Teaching Points	Organisation	Duration
Entry: swivel entry	hold the side with both hands	all together	1 min
Warm up: 2 widths any stroke with buoyancy aids	take your time	all together	3 mins
Main Theme: 2 widths full stroke breaststroke	pull in a circle and kick in a circle	all together	3 mins
sitting on the poolside demonstrating arm action	scoop around in a circle shape	all together	3 mins
walking though the water using arm action	pull the water apart	all together	3 mins
arm action with a noodle under the arms	pull in a *small* circle	all together	3 mins
arms and legs with noodle under the arms	stretch arms out front	all together	3 mins
full stroke with buoyancy aids if necessary	pull around and stretch	all together	3 mins
Contrasting Activity: supine star float	look up and relax	one by one	3 mins
swimming through a partially submerged hoop	eyes open	one by one	3 mins
Exit: using the pool steps or over the poolside	take your time	one by one	1 min

Total time: 29 minutes

Lesson #10 Assessment

Lesson Objective: to learn and practice basic breaststroke arm pull.		
Below average	**Average**	**Above average**
😐	🙂	😎
Attempts to demonstrate but does not show the correct technique	**Able to perform most of the technique correctly some of the time**	**Performs the technique correctly most of the time**

Assessment	😐	🙂	😎
Arm pulls are simultaneous			
Elbows bend and tuck in			
Fingers are together			
Arms stretch forwards			

Lesson Plan #11

Lesson type: breaststroke arms
Level: adult or child intermediate
Previous learning: basic breaststroke technique
Lesson aim: to develop and progress breaststroke arm technique
Equipment: floats and/or woggles and sinkers

Exercise/Activity	Teaching Points	Organisation	Duration
Entry: swivel entry or sitting dive entry	take your time	all together	1 min
Warm up: 2 widths any stroke	continuous swimming	all together	2 mins
Main Theme: 2 widths full stroke breaststroke	pull in a circle and kick in a circle	all together	3 mins
arm action with a woggle under the arms	fingers together	waves	3 mins
arms pulls with woggle under the arms, adding breathing	stretch forwards	waves	3 mins
push and glide adding arm pulls	pull in a *small* circle	waves	3 mins
push and glide adding alternate arm pull, leg kick action in slow motion	keep hands in front of the shoulders	all together	3 mins
full stroke breaststroke	hands together when gliding	all together	3 mins
Contrasting Activity: treading water	mouth and nose out of the water	one by one	2 mins
retrieve an object from the pool floor and return it to the poolside	eyes open	one by one	4 mins
Exit: using the pool steps or over the poolside	take your time	one by one	1 min

Total time: 28 minutes

Lesson #11 Assessment

Lesson Objective: to progress basic breaststroke arm action and introduce breathing.		
Below average	**Average**	**Above average**
😐	🙂	😎
Attempts to demonstrate but does not show the correct technique	**Able to perform most of the technique correctly some of the time**	**Performs the technique correctly most of the time**

Assessment	😐	🙂	😎
Arms pull in a small circle			
Elbows bend and tuck in			
Fingers are together			
Arms stretch forwards into a glide			

Lesson Plan #12

Lesson type: breaststroke arms
Level: adult or child advanced
Previous learning: full stroke breaststroke
Lesson aim: to develop and fine-tune breaststroke arm action
Equipment: hand paddles

Exercise/Activity	Teaching Points	Organisation	Duration
Entry: sitting or shallow dive entry	take your time	waves	1 min
Warm up: 2 lengths any stroke	take your time	all together	3 mins
Main Theme: 2 lengths full stroke breaststroke	let your movements flow	waves	3 mins
push and glide adding arm pulls	hands in front of shoulders	waves	3 mins
push and glide adding arm pulls, with hand paddles	tuck your elbows in and stretch	waves	3 mins
full stroke with hand paddles	pull with power	waves	3 mins
1 length full stroke counting strokes	pull and stretch	waves	3 mins
2 lengths full stroke breaststroke	pull, breathe, kick, glide	waves	3 mins
Contrasting Activity: feet first sculling	feet remain at the surface	waves	3 mins
basic racing start	head tucked down on entry	one at a time	3 mins
Exit: using the pool steps or over the poolside	take your time	waves	1 min

Total time: 29 minutes

Lesson #12 Assessment

Lesson Objective: to develop and fine-tune breaststroke arm action.		
Below average	**Average**	**Above average**
😐	🙂	😎
Attempts to demonstrate but does not show the correct technique	Able to perform most of the technique correctly some of the time	Performs the technique correctly most of the time

Assessment	😐	🙂	😎
Arms pull in a small circle			
Elbows bend and tuck in			
Fingers are together throughout			
Hands remain in front of the shoulders			
Arms stretch forwards into a glide			

Lesson Plan #13
Lesson type: breaststroke breathing
Level: adult or child beginner
Previous learning: basic front paddle and submerging
Lesson aim: to learn basic breaststroke breathing technique
Equipment: floats, kickboards and buoyancy aids as necessary

Exercise/Activity	Teaching Points	Organisation	Duration
Entry: pool steps or swivel entry	enter slowly	all together	1 min
Warm up: 2 widths any stroke using buoyancy aids	take your time	all together	2 mins
Main Theme: standing in water, breathing with arm action	breathe through your mouth	all together	2 mins
walking through the water using arms and breathing	blow your hands forwards	waves	3 mins
woggle held under the arms with arm pulls with breathing	face up as you breathe in	waves	3 mins
floats under each arm, kick and breathe out	face down as you breathe out	waves	4 mins
woggle under the arms, full stroke performed slowly with breathing	pull your head up, kick your head down	all together	3 mins
full stroke with breathing (use buoyancy aids if necessary)	breathe out into a glide	all together	3 mins
Contrasting Activity: pencil jump	jump away from the side	all together	2 mins
tuck float (timed)	deep breath, chin to chest	all together	2 mins
Exit: using the pool steps	take your time	one by one	1 min

Total time: 26 minutes

Lesson #13 Assessment

Lesson Objective: to introduce basic breaststroke breathing technique.		
Below average	**Average**	**Above average**
😐	🙂	😎
Attempts to demonstrate but does not show the correct technique	**Able to perform most of the technique correctly some of the time**	**Performs the technique correctly most of the time**

Assessment	😐	🙂	😎
Head is in a central position			
Face up to inhale			
Face down to exhale			
Breathing takes place through the mouth			

Lesson Plan #14

Lesson type: breaststroke breathing
Level: adult or child intermediate
Previous learning: basic breaststroke technique
Lesson aim: to develop and progress breaststroke breathing technique
Equipment: floats and/or kickboards

Exercise/Activity	Teaching Points	Organisation	Duration
Entry: swivel or sitting dive entry	enter slowly	waves/ all together	1 min
Warm up: 2 widths any stroke	take your time	all together	3 mins
Main Theme: full stroke with breathing (use buoyancy aids if necessary)	breathe through your mouth	all together	3 mins
arms pulls with a woggle	blow your hands forwards	waves	3 mins
woggle under the arms, full stroke performed slowly with breathing	pull, breathe, kick, blow	waves	3 mins
1 float held in front, kick and breathe out	kick and blow	waves	3 mins
push and glide, adding 'pull, breathe, kick, blow' sequence	kick and blow your hands forwards	waves	3 mins
2 widths full stroke breaststroke	breathe out as you glide	waves	3 mins
Contrasting Activity: treading water	ears above the water	all together	2 mins
head first sculling	look up at the sky	waves	3 mins
Exit: using the pool steps	take your time	one by one	1 min

Total time: 28 minutes

Lesson #14 Assessment

Lesson Objective: to develop and progress basic breaststroke breathing technique.		
Below average	**Average**	**Above average**
😐	🙂	😎
Attempts to demonstrate but does not show the correct technique	**Able to perform most of the technique correctly some of the time**	**Performs the technique correctly most of the time**

Assessment	😐	🙂	😎
Head is in a central position			
Inhale as the arms pull			
Exhale as the legs kick			
Breathing takes place through the mouth			
Exhalation continues through the glide			

Lesson Plan #15

Lesson type: breaststroke breathing
Level: adult or child advanced
Previous learning: full stroke breaststroke
Lesson aim: to develop and perfect breaststroke breathing technique
Equipment: floats and/or kickboard if needed

Exercise/Activity	Teaching Points	Organisation	Duration
Entry: sitting or shallow dive entry	take your time	waves	1 min
Warm up: 2 lengths any stroke	take your time	all together	3 mins
Main Theme: 2 lengths full stroke breaststroke	let the stroke movements flow	all together	3 mins
1 length full stroke, counting strokes	breathe out into the glide	waves	3 mins
1 length, 2 stroke cycles per breath	breathe out slowly	waves	3 mins
repeat previous drill, try to reduce the number of stroke cycles	control your breath out	waves	3 mins
1 length full stroke against the clock, using head movement to gain momentum	breathe out with power	waves	3 mins
2 lengths full stroke breaststroke	breathe out, glide and stretch	waves	3 mins
Contrasting Activity: treading water - vary with 1 arm behind the back or above the water	ears and mouth above the surface	waves	3 mins
basic racing start	push hard from the legs	waves	3 mins
Exit: using the pool steps or over the poolside	take your time	one by one	1 min

Total time: 29 minutes

Lesson #15 Assessment

Lesson Objective: to develop and perfect breaststroke breathing technique.		
Below average	**Average**	**Above average**
😐	🙂	😎
Attempts to demonstrate but does not show the correct technique	**Able to perform most of the technique correctly some of the time**	**Performs the technique correctly most of the time**

Assessment	😐	🙂	😎
Head is in a central position			
Inhale as the arms pull			
Exhale as the legs kick			
Breathing takes place through the mouth			
Exhalation is continuous and unlabored			
Head dive is used to gain momentum			

Lesson Plan #16

Lesson type: breaststroke timing and coordination

Level: adult or child beginners
Previous learning: basic breaststroke arm pull and leg kick
Lesson aim: to learn basic breaststroke timing and coordination
Equipment: floats, buoyancy aids and sinkers

Exercise/Activity	Teaching Points	Organisation	Duration
Entry: swivel entry or use pool steps	enter slowly	all together	1 min
Warm up: 2 widths full stroke breaststroke, with aids if needed	pull then kick	all together	3 mins
Main Theme: Push and glide with a streamlined shape	hands together	all together	2 mins
Push and glide, adding leg kicks	kick and glide	waves	3 mins
Push and glide adding arm pulls	Pull around and stretch forward	waves	3 mins
Push and glide adding arm pulls and leg kicks	pull, kick and glide	waves	3 mins
Repeat previous exercise, adding breathing	pull, breathe and kick	waves	3 mins
Full stroke breaststroke, swum slowly	pull, breathe, kick, glide	one by one	4 mins
Contrasting Activity: pencil jump	jump away from the poolside	one by one	2 mins
retrieve sinkers	deep breath and dig deep	one by one	3 mins
Exit: Using the pool steps	take your time	one by one	1 min

Total time: 28 minutes

Lesson #16 Assessment

Lesson Objective: to introduce a basic breaststroke timing pattern.		
Below average	**Average**	**Above average**
😐	🙂	😎
Attempts to demonstrate but does not show the correct technique	Able to perform most of the technique correctly some of the time	Performs the technique correctly most of the time

Assessment	😐	🙂	😎
Leg kicks are simultaneous and circular			
Arm pulls are simultaneous and circular			
Pull *then* kick			
Glide after each kick			

Lesson Plan #17

Lesson type: breaststroke timing and coordination

Level: adult or child intermediate
Previous learning: basic timing technique
Lesson aim: to progress and develop previous learning of breaststroke timing
Equipment: floats if needed and hoop

Exercise/Activity	Teaching Points	Organisation	Duration
Entry: swivel or sitting dive entry	enter slowly	waves/ all together	1 min
Warm up: 2 widths any stroke	take your time	all together	3 mins
Main Theme: 2 widths full stroke breaststroke	swim with smooth movements	all together	2 mins
Push and glide with a streamlined shape	stretch and glide	waves	3 mins
push and glide, adding arm pulls and leg kicks	pull then kick	waves	3 mins
repeat previous drill, adding breaths	pull, breath, kick	waves	3 mins
push and glide, adding the stroke sequence and returning to a glide	kick into a glide	waves	3 mins
1 length full stroke breaststroke	pull, breathe, kick and glide	waves	3 mins
Contrasting Activity: feet first surface dives through a submerged hoop	stretch up and sink	one by one	4 mins
feet first sculling	toes at the surface	waves	3 mins
Exit: using the pool steps	take your time	one by one	1 min

Total time: 29 minutes

Lesson #17 Assessment

Lesson Objective: to progress and develop previous learning of breaststroke timing.		
Below average	**Average**	**Above average**
😐	🙂	😎
Attempts to demonstrate but does not show the correct technique	**Able to perform most of the technique correctly some of the time**	**Performs the technique correctly most of the time**

Assessment	😐	🙂	😎
Arm pulls are followed by a breath			
Legs kick into a glide			
Pull *then* kick			
Glide after each kick			

Lesson Plan #18

Lesson type: breaststroke timing and coordination

Level: adult or child advanced
Previous learning: full stroke breaststroke
Lesson aim: to develop and fine-tune breaststroke timing
Equipment: floats and sinkers if needed

Exercise/Activity	Teaching Points	Organisation	Duration
Entry: sitting or shallow dive entry	take your time	waves	1 min
Warm up: 2 lengths any stroke	take your time	all together	3 mins
Main Theme: 2 lengths full stroke breaststroke	smooth flowing stroke	all together	2 mins
full stroke, 2 leg kicks to 1 arm pull	kick and glide	waves	3 mins
1 length counting stroke cycles	kick into the glide	one by one	3 mins
1 length counting stroke cycles, reduce the number of cycles per length	maximise your glide	one by one	3 mins
2 lengths full stroke maintaining the reduced stroke rate from previous	smooth strokes and glide	waves	3 mins
2 lengths full stroke breaststroke	pull, breathe, kick and glide	waves	3 mins
Contrasting Activity: head first surface dive and swim underwater for a pre-set distance	deep breath and dig down deep	one by one	3 mins
basic grab start	fast transition to stroke	waves	3 mins
Exit: using the pool steps	take your time	one by one	1 min

Total time: 28 minutes

Lesson #18 Assessment

Lesson Objective: to develop and fine-tune breaststroke timing.

Below average	Average	Above average
😐	🙂	😎
Attempts to demonstrate but does not show the correct technique	Able to perform most of the technique correctly some of the time	Performs the technique correctly most of the time

Assessment	😐	🙂	😎
Kick into a glide			
Pull *then* kick			
Glide after each kick			
Attempts to maximise the glide			
Reduce or maintain stroke rate			

"Now that you have finished my book, would you please consider writing a review? Reviews are the best way readers discover great new books. I would truly appreciate it."

Mark Young

For more information about teaching swimming, learning to swim and improving swimming technique visit **Swim Teach**.

"The number one resource for learning to swim
and improving swimming technique."

www.swim-teach.com

Printed in Great Britain
by Amazon

84698892R00072